Cambridge **Discovery Education**™

▶ **INTERACTIVE READERS**

Series editor: Bob Hastings

THE WHEEL

A2+

Caroline Shackleton and Nathan Paul Turner

CAMBRIDGE UNIVERSITY PRESS
Cambridge, New York, Melbourne, Madrid, Cape Town,
Singapore, São Paulo, Delhi, Mexico City

Cambridge University Press
32 Avenue of the Americas, New York, NY 10013-2473, USA

www.cambridge.org
Information on this title: www.cambridge.org/9781107667396

First published 2014

Printed in Hong Kong, China, by Golden Cup Printing Company Limited

A catalog record for this publication is available from the British Library.

Library of Congress Cataloging-in-Publication Data

Shackleton, Caroline.
 The wheel / Caroline Shackleton and Nathan Paul Turner.
    pages cm. -- (Cambridge discovery interactive readers)
  ISBN 978-1-107-66739-6 (pbk. : alk. paper)
1. Wheels--Juvenile literature. 2. English language--Textbooks for foreign speakers. 3. Readers
(Elementary) I. Title.

TJ181.5.S43 2013
621.8--dc23

                                    2013025123

ISBN 978-1-107-66739-6

Additional resources for this publication at www.cambridge.org

Layout services, art direction, book design, and photo research: Q2ABillSMITH GROUP
Editorial services: Hyphen S.A.
Audio production: CityVox, New York
Video production: Q2ABillSMITH GROUP

Contents

Before You Read:
Get Ready!

Wheels make the world go round! But this wasn't always true. It took early people a long time to invent the wheel. Some say that this first big idea is still our best idea. Is the wheel man's greatest invention?

Words to Know

Look at the pictures. Then complete the definitions below with the correct words.

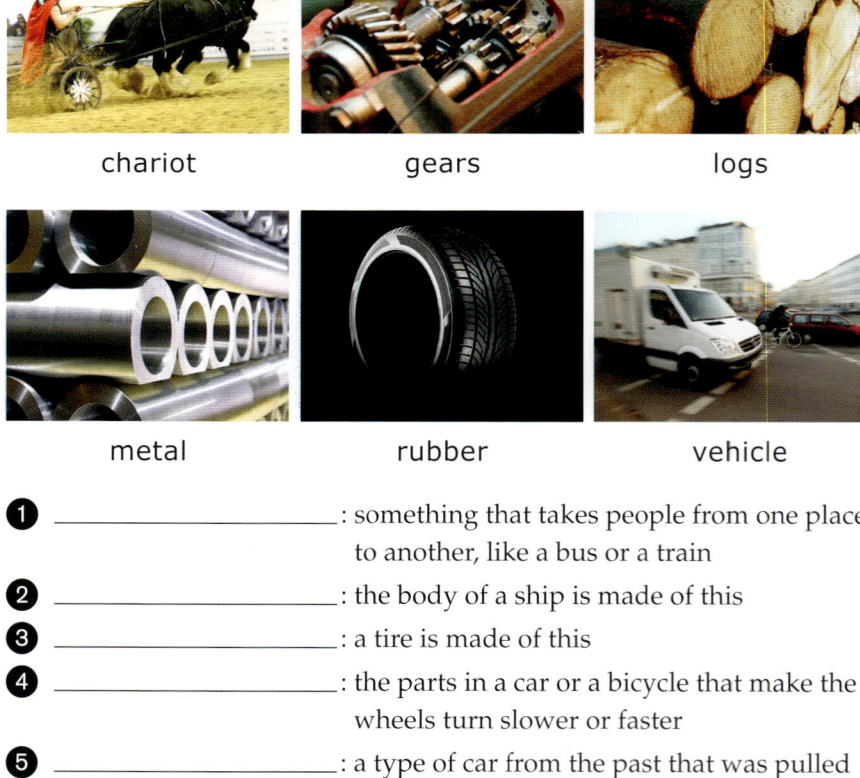

chariot   gears   logs

metal   rubber   vehicle

1 _____ : something that takes people from one place to another, like a bus or a train

2 _____ : the body of a ship is made of this

3 _____ : a tire is made of this

4 _____ : the parts in a car or a bicycle that make the wheels turn slower or faster

5 _____ : a type of car from the past that was pulled by horses

6 _____ : long, round pieces of a tree

Words to Know

Read the article. Then complete the definitions below with the correct highlighted words.

What is a wheel?

The wheel is a very important invention. It is round and can turn and roll over different kinds of ground, so wheels make transportation easier. Wheeled vehicles like cars, buses, trains, or bikes carry people or things quickly and comfortably. On most vehicles the front wheels turn left and right. This lets the driver steer the vehicle. The power that drives most of these vehicles comes from gas or electricity, but the power that pushes the bicycle comes from your legs!

1 _____: change the direction of a vehicle

2 _____: something made for the first time

3 _____: what our feet walk on

4 _____: energy

5 _____: the way people or things are moved from one place to another

6 _____: move by turning over and over

Look at the diagram. How do you say these words in your language?

? PREDICT
How and when was the wheel invented?

tire

spokes

axle

brakes

CHAPTER 1

Inventing the Wheel

IT'S A MAN-MADE INVENTION, IT HAS COMPLETELY CHANGED THE WAY WE LIVE, AND IT'S EVERYWHERE IN THE WORLD. WHAT IS IT? THE WHEEL!

Wheels are all around us. You use them every day, but you probably don't think about them very often. In fact, the wheel as we know it is quite a new **invention**.

There are no real wheels in nature. There aren't any animals that use wheels to get around. But why not? Why are there no animals with wheels instead of legs? Perhaps because wheels aren't any good on some kinds of ground. It's hard to cross the desert or the forest or to climb a mountain on wheels. However, for humans, the wheel has been an amazing invention.

If there are no wheels in nature, how did people first make them? Nobody really knows the answer. There are many round shapes and circles in nature, but they aren't like wheels; they aren't used to help move things.

The earliest people worked with **stone**. So, maybe they saw round stones rolling. But they also made boats from wood. Perhaps they saw the logs they used for building boats rolling down a hill!

One of the earliest uses of logs to move things was in Egypt about 3000 BCE. Logs were used to build the pyramids. The heavy stones for these buildings were put on flat sleds and pulled forward over logs, called rollers. The rolling logs helped move the stones more easily.

The first wheels were solid wood.

The first real wheels were probably made in Mesopotamia, now Iraq. But **scientists** think that those first wheels were not used for moving a vehicle. They were used in pottery wheels. These machines turned quickly in a circle to help people make things like cups and bowls. Another early wheel, a millstone, was a heavy, round stone. It was used for breaking down plants for cooking and for making flour.[1]

The earliest pictures of wheels on vehicles are on Mesopotamian paintings from 3000–2700 BCE. These wheels were made of solid[2] wood and turned on a simple axle. Around 2000 BCE the Egyptians started using spokes on their chariot wheels. These wheels needed less wood, so they were cheaper to make. They were also much lighter and could travel faster.

[1]**flour:** used to make bread, cakes, etc.
[2]**solid:** without any holes or openings

The wheel was soon used by different groups of people across Europe and Asia. By 500 BCE, many types of wheeled vehicles were in use, from fast chariots to large, slow carts.[3] The wheels they used are much like the wheels we use today.

However, in other places in the world, wheels were never used. Central and South American peoples, like the Mayans or Incas, built amazing cities and temples without using wheels. Nobody knows why, but it may be because they lived in mountainous areas, where it was impossible to use wheeled vehicles.

A Mayan temple

Wheels are no good in high mountains, in deep snow, or in desert sands. Even today in the Sahara desert, animals like the camel are more useful than wheeled vehicles.

[3]**cart:** a vehicle with two or four wheels that is pushed by a person or pulled by an animal
[4]**all-terrain vehicle:** a vehicle that can travel on many different kinds of ground

Video Quest

Legs or Wheels: part 1

Watch this video about some men trying to make a new kind of all-terrain vehicle.[4] What is the idea behind the new invention?

CHAPTER 2

Making Wheels Work

THE WHEEL IS BEST KNOWN FOR ITS USE IN VEHICLES, BUT IT WAS FIRST USED IN INDUSTRY.

Throughout history machines have used wheels. And for a long time wheels also made machines work. The first wheel used for **power** was the waterwheel. This was a great improvement in **technology** because it let people use running water to power machines instead of using animals or other people.

The first waterwheel we know about was in a flour mill in Byzantium, now Turkey. The first waterwheels lay on their sides. But by 240 CE, in Alexandria in Egypt, people were using wheels that stood up in rivers and were much more powerful.

To use waterwheels to drive machines, people needed a way to send the power from the turning wheel to the things they wanted to work on. They used more wheels! They found that if you cut teeth into two wheels and put them together, the first wheel turns the second one.

As early as 330 BCE, the Greek inventor Archimedes talked about toothed wheels, called gears. He **realized** that when the teeth from the first wheel push the second, the second wheel turns in the opposite direction. But a third wheel moves opposite to the second, in the same direction as the first one. By putting gears together, you can send the power from a waterwheel to a machine. The Greeks used gears to make complicated mechanisms[5] like clocks.

[5]**mechanism:** one part of a machine that does a special job

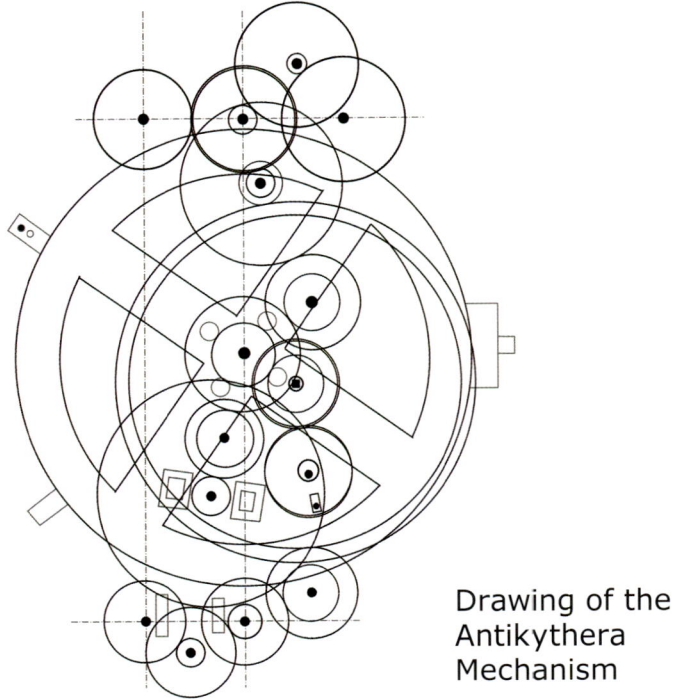

Drawing of the Antikythera Mechanism

Perhaps the most **complicated** early use of gears that we know about is the Antikythera Mechanism. It was found under the sea in a shipwreck[6] near the Greek Island of Antikythera in 1901. There was a case with instructions in Greek, 30 gears, and 82 pieces made of the metal bronze.

Scientists thought that these pieces were part of a very complicated kind of clock, but it took them almost 100 years to put the pieces together! In fact, the Antikythera was a planetarium, a machine that shows the movements of the planets[7] and the moon around the sun. It was actually a kind of calendar. It showed scientists that the ancient world had complicated technology and knew a lot about space.

[6]**shipwreck:** a ship that sank in an accident
[7]**planets:** very big, round things, like Earth, that move around a star

Another important wheel for **industry** was the windmill. Windmills use sails to catch the wind and make power. Unfortunately, windmills only work if it's windy! But they have one great advantage. Waterwheels need rivers, but you can build a windmill anywhere that's windy. Modern windmills, called wind turbines, are used as a clean way to make electricity.

A windmill with sails

Finally, steam power, the key to the Industrial Revolution,[8] also used the wheel. Steam from boiling water moved wheels and powered machines. From the 17th century, steam power was seen more and more in mills and factories. By the 19th century, steam was powering the new trains and ships and driving forward trade[9] and industry. The age of industrial power had begun!

A steam engine

[8] **Industrial Revolution:** the time in history when machines in big factories started doing a lot of work
[9] **trade:** buying and selling things

?

UNDERSTAND
Describe two ways wheels were used in the past.

A bucket wheel excavator moving earth

CHAPTER 3

A World Full of Wheels!

WE SEE WHEELS EVERYWHERE WE LOOK.

Wheels make modern transportation possible. There are big wheels, small wheels, fast wheels, slow wheels. Let's take a look at some facts about wheels, and some of the inventions that have made them better.

Small wheels

The smallest motor vehicle you can drive on a road is the Peel P50. It was first built in the 1960s on the Isle of Man between England and Ireland, but only 50 were made. The P50 had only three wheels, was very light, and had just one front light and one door. It could only drive forward. If you wanted to go backward, you had to pull it by hand. But it was small enough to keep in your house!

An articulated truck

Big wheels

The biggest vehicle in the world is the bucket-wheel excavator. These machines use very big wheels to move large pieces of earth. The biggest, the Bagger 293, is 96 meters tall and 225 meters long, and it weighs 142,000 kilograms! Its wheel is 21 meters across! But it can only move very slowly, traveling just half a kilometer an hour!

Lots of wheels

The road vehicle with the most wheels is the articulated truck. These big, heavy vehicles carry food, animals, gas, and many other things. They often have five axles and eighteen wheels and are sometimes known as 18-wheelers. Only the front two wheels are like the wheels on a normal car. The other sixteen wheels sit in pairs on four of the axles. This makes the vehicle safer.

The Bugatti Veyron

Fast wheels

Horses pull a heavy vehicle at about 3 kilometers an hour. The first modern cars at the end of the 19th century could go 40 or 50 kilometers an hour. Today, the fastest factory-built road car in the world is the Bugatti Veyron. Its engine has the same power as 1,200 horses, and it can go 431 kilometers an hour! Only 300 Veyrons were made, and buying one will cost you $2,350,000!

Slow wheels

It's good to go fast if you know how to stop! Because motor vehicles like trains and cars go so fast, they need brakes to slow them down and make them safe. Brakes need to be very strong. Those in a normal car today are made to take temperatures of over 230°C!

Comfortable wheels

Driving with wooden wheels isn't much fun. Thankfully, today's vehicles have suspension. The car sits on springs to make the ride softer and more comfortable. They also use air-filled rubber tires, which were **invented** in 1887. Today, about 1.3 billion car tires are sold around the world every year!

Steering wheels

How many wheels does a car have? Four? Don't forget the fifth wheel – the **steering wheel**. Nowadays, many cars use power steering to help the driver. When the steering wheel is turned, the car uses a computer and motors to turn the front wheels. This makes steering heavier vehicles much easier than before. Imagine trying to steer an 18-wheeler truck by yourself!

A car suspension with springs

The first bicycle pedals were on the front wheel.

Pushing wheels

How can you use your legs to move but travel five times faster than walking? Ride a bike! The bicycle was invented at the end of the 19th century. Cyclists push, or pedal, the wheels around with the power of their legs. The first pedals were on the front wheel, but this was dangerous, so the pedals were moved to the middle of the bicycle.

A tandem bike

Today there are many different types of bicycles. Road bikes travel fast on thin tires, while mountain bikes have fat, strong tires and can travel off-road. Couples can cycle tandems – long bikes with two seats and four pedals. And some people can even ride unicycles – cycles with only one wheel!

A unicycle

Video Quest

Legs or Wheels: part 2

Watch the next part of this video. How many legs does their invention have?

Changing wheels

Have you ever tried to pedal a bike up a big hill? It can be very hard if you don't use the right gear. Nowadays most bikes have different gears for going faster or slower. Racing bikes and mountain bikes can have 21 or more gears. Of course, these gears are also wheels!

Tough[10] wheels

Although normal wheels can travel over many types of road, they can have problems with softer ground or snow. One way to help them is to give them their own moving "road." Many big vehicles like tanks have their wheels inside special tracks made of metal or rubber, which make it easier to go on difficult ground. These tough wheels can go almost anywhere!

[10] **tough:** strong and not easily broken

A tank

CHAPTER 4

Fun with Wheels!

WHEELS ARE ALSO USED FOR FUN!

Sports

Nowadays, some of the most popular and exciting sports are wheeled sports. Almost every vehicle you can think of is used for racing. There are long-distance bike races such as the Tour de France, which goes about 3,400 kilometers through France and lasts for three weeks! There are high-speed sports such as Moto GP motorcycle racing, or the Formula 1 Grand Prix races, where cars drive up to 350 kilometers per hour.

But high-speed racing is nothing new. The Ancient Greeks and Romans loved watching high-speed chariot races. Chariot races were an important part of the Greek Olympic Games. Chariot racing was very dangerous, and the drivers often died, but the winners could become very rich! A bit like Formula 1 today.

Games and Toys

Wheels have been part of children's toys for thousands of years. The ancient Mayan people did not use wheeled vehicles, but they made small toy animals with wheels. The ancient Greeks also had small wheeled animal toys for their children.

Hoops – thin wheels made of metal, wood, or plastic – have been popular for a very long time. Children in China played with them thousands of years ago, and in ancient Greece children rolled bronze hoops. From the Middle Ages until the 20th century, wooden hoops were used in games in many countries.

Some groups of Native Americans have hoop dances, using as many as 30 hoops at once! In their dances the hoop shows the circle of life.

Hoop dancing is also popular today, not only for fun, but also as a way of keeping fit.

A Native American hoop dancer

The Singapore Flyer is the highest Ferris wheel in the world.

Amusement[11] rides

A good way to have fun on wheels is to go on a ride in a fair or amusement park.

Roller coasters are like trains except they're much more exciting. They go up and down and turn really fast to make the passengers afraid, excited, and sometimes sick! The fastest roller coaster in the world is the Ferrari Formula Rossi in Dubai. It can go 240 kilometers per hour!

Another fun wheel is the Ferris wheel. Invented by George Ferris in 1893 in the USA, these giant[12] wheels don't go fast. In fact, they turn slowly. But they're really high, so passengers can enjoy amazing views. The highest Ferris wheel in the world is the Singapore Flyer. It is 165 meters high!

[11] **amusement:** something that you do for fun
[12] **giant:** very big

Skates and skateboards

What do you call boots with four wheels? Roller skates! They were invented in 1760 and had two wheels on each side of the boot. But they didn't become popular until the end of the 19th century.

In the 20th century, roller skates became really popular. They were used in races, games, and for dancing to disco music! Now inline skates are more popular. They have four wheels under the boot. This makes them go faster, but it also makes it easier to fall down!

Roller disco

You can surf in the sea, but can you surf on roads? You can if you have a skateboard. Skateboards were invented in California, USA, in the 1950s, when some surfers put wheels on their surfboards!

Inline skaters

Skateboarders today do amazing things and go really fast. The fastest skateboarder in the world went 130 kilometers per hour!

A skateboarder

? EVALUATE
Which activity do you think is the most dangerous? Why?

CHAPTER 5

What Do You Think?

DON'T REINVENT THE WHEEL!

We often tell people "don't reinvent the wheel." This means we think they are wasting their time by inventing something that we already have. The idea is that the wheel is so good, you can't make it any better. But what if nobody in history ever reinvented the wheel? Maybe our cars would travel on logs.

Sometimes, it is a good idea to reinvent the wheel. Just because an invention is good, doesn't mean we can't make it better, faster, or lighter.

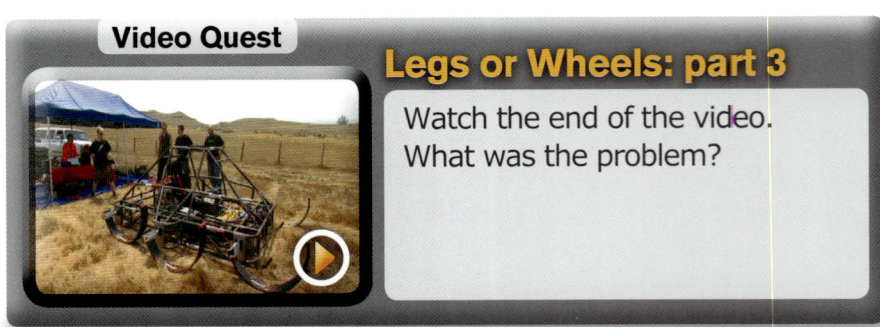

Video Quest

Legs or Wheels: part 3

Watch the end of the video. What was the problem?

Look at the inventions in the table. Say how they have been reinvented and the good and bad things about the reinventions.

Invention	Reinvention	Good things	Bad things
telephones	cell phones	can be carried in your pocket; can send text messages	can be noisy in public places; people can always find you
light bulbs			
maps			
stairs			
music records			
books			
typewriters			

How have the inventions in the table changed our lives? Which is your favorite invention? Your favorite reinvention? Why?

After You Read

Read the questions and choose Ⓐ, Ⓑ, or Ⓒ.

❶ What are millstones used for?

Ⓐ to travel
Ⓑ to move things
Ⓒ to make flour

❷ What was the first water-powered wheel used for?

Ⓐ to transport things
Ⓑ to cut wood
Ⓒ to power machines

❸ How are windmills better than watermills?

Ⓐ They can be built anywhere.
Ⓑ They can make power.
Ⓒ They are cheaper to build.

❹ How many Peel P50's were built?

Ⓐ fewer than 100
Ⓑ more than 100
Ⓒ exactly 100

❺ Why did the Ancient Greeks take part in races?

Ⓐ to make money
Ⓑ to become kings
Ⓒ to show they were brave

❻ What did Mayan children play with?

Ⓐ toy chariots
Ⓑ wooden hoops
Ⓒ wheeled toy animals

Read the sentences and choose Ⓐ (True) or Ⓑ (False).

1 We know that the first wheel was invented by the Mayans.

   Ⓐ True

   Ⓑ False

2 The pyramids were built using stone wheels.

   Ⓐ True

   Ⓑ False

3 Camels are sometimes better than wheels for difficult terrain.

   Ⓐ True

   Ⓑ False

4 A shipwreck taught us that the ancient world knew a lot about the planets.

   Ⓐ True

   Ⓑ False

5 Tanks can move over difficult ground because the wheels are inside tracks.

   Ⓐ True

   Ⓑ False

6 The position of bicycle pedals was changed to save money.

   Ⓐ True

   Ⓑ False

7 Hoops are used as a form of exercise.

   Ⓐ True

   Ⓑ False

8 Roller skates became popular as soon as they were invented.

   Ⓐ True

   Ⓑ False

Answer Key

Words to Know, page 4

1 vehicle **2** metal **3** rubber **4** gears **5** chariot
6 logs

Words to Know, page 5

1 steer **2** invention **3** ground **4** power
5 transportation **6** roll

Predict, page 5

Answers will vary.

Video Quest, page 9

To have a vehicle that moves like animals or insects
with legs.

Understand, page 13

Answers will vary.

Video Quest, page 19

Six legs

Evaluate, page 23

Answers will vary.

Video Quest, page 24

The body was too heavy.

Choose the Correct Answers, page 26

1 C **2** C **3** A **4** A **5** A **6** C

True or False? page 27

1 B **2** B **3** A **4** A **5** A **6** B **7** A **8** B